For Grades
1&2

Student Workbook

Write
on Target

Using Graphic Organizers
to Improve Writing Skills

Written By:
Yolande F. Grizinski, Ed.D.
Leslie Holzhauser-Peters, MS, CCC-SP

Show What You Know
Publishing

Acknowledgements

Show What You Know® Publishing acknowledges the following for their efforts in making this material available for students, parents, and teachers.

Cindi Englefield, President/Publisher
Eloise Boehm-Sasala, Vice President/Managing Editor
Mercedes Baltzell, Production Editor
Scott D. Stuckey, Editor
Lainie Burke, Desktop Publisher/Assistant Editor
Jennifer Harney, Illustrator/Cover Designer

Content Reviewers:
Kathie Christian, Proofreader
Erica T. Klingerman, Proofreader

Printer:
McNaughton & Gunn, Inc.

Published by:
Show What You Know® Publishing
A Division of Englefield & Associates, Inc.
P.O. Box 341348
6344 Nicholas Drive
Columbus, OH 43234-1348
(614) 764-1211
www.showwhatyouknowpublishing.com

Printed in the United States of America
09 08 07 06   20 19 18 17 16 15 14 13 12 11 10 9 8 7 6 5 4 3 2

ISBN   1-884183-94-8

About the Authors

Yolande F. Grizinski received a Bachelor's degree from Miami University, a Master's degree from Wright State University, and a Doctor of Education from the University of Cincinnati. She has worked in public education for 28 years as a curriculum consultant in the areas of language arts with a focus on writing assessment. She is currently the Assistant Superintendent of the Warren County Educational Service Center in Lebanon, Ohio.

Leslie Holzhauser-Peters holds a Bachelor's degree from the University of Cincinnati and Master's degree from Miami University. She has 25 years of experience working in public schools in Special Education and as a Speech-language pathologist, as a Supervisor, and currently as a Curriculum Consultant. Her areas of expertise are language, literacy, and intervention.

The authors met at the Warren County Educational Service Center in Lebanon, Ohio. There they developed and implemented a host of language arts initiatives including a large-scale writing assessment. They have given numerous presentations on the five communication processes and Ohio's proficiencies.

Table of Contents

Chapter 1

Narrative
(Fictional Narrative, Personal Experience Narrative, and Retelling)

What is a Narrative?

The purpose of a narrative is to tell a story.

A **fictional narrative** is a made-up story. Fictional narratives are not true.

In a **personal experience narrative**, you write about something that has happened to you, or something that could have happened to you in real life.

A **retelling** tells the story again in your own words.

Writing Activity 1: Fictional Narrative
(A Made-Up Story)

Step 1 Follow along as the fictional narrative (a made-up story) "Wuffy" is read aloud.

Wuffy

Wuffy was a cute little puppy. He had brown fur and brown eyes. He loved to bark at other dogs, play with his toys, chase his tail, and do all kinds of cute "doggy" things. Some people might have thought Wuffy was a very happy puppy. But Wuffy was sad.

Wuffy's home was behind bars in a loud, stinky place called the pound. He wanted to be adopted, and he would have done whatever it took to find a home.

Human after human walked by his cage. Wuffy cried and howled in his loudest bark. "Pick me!" he cried, but no one picked Wuffy.

Wuffy was so tired and sad that he fell asleep on his torn blanket.

While he was sleeping, a young boy visited the pound. He was looking for the perfect puppy. He looked in Wuffy's cage and saw the sleeping dog.

"I'll take this one," the boy said. Wuffy was adopted.

by Alexandra Grizinski

Step **2**   Remember, a good fictional narrative (a made-up story) has the following parts.

- a title
- a character or characters you can picture in your mind
- a problem
- a beginning, a middle, and an end

Step **3**   Use the following idea to plan your fictional narrative (a made-up story).

> **Tell your teacher a story about your favorite animal. It can be your stuffed animal toy, an animal you have seen, or even a pet.**

Step **4**   Answer the planning questions to get ideas for your made-up story. Use your picture board or graphic organizer to help you think through your fictional narrative (a made-up story). You can use pictures or words to plan your fictional narrative (a made-up story).

FICTIONAL NARRATIVE

Planning Questions for a Made-Up Story

Use pictures or words.

Who are the characters?

Where does the story take place?

When does the story happen?

What happens in the story?

How does the story end?

FICTIONAL NARRATIVE

Picture Board for a Made-Up Story

Beginning:

Middle:

End:

FICTIONAL NARRATIVE

Graphic Organizer for a Made-Up Story

Title: _____

Beginning:

Middle:

End:

Write your fictional narrative (a made-up story).

Writing Activity 1

Step

5

If you need more room, ask a parent or a teacher for another piece of paper.

Step
6
The checklist shows what your best paper must have. Use the checklist below to review your work.

Checklist for Writing Activity 1

❏ My story has a title.

❏ My story is a made-up story.

❏ My characters have names.

❏ My story has a beginning, a middle, and an end.

❏ I try to spell words correctly.

❏ My sentences end with a period, an exclamation point, or a question mark.

❏ My sentences begin with capital letters.

Writing Activity 2: Fictional Narrative
(A Made-Up Story)

Step **1** Follow along as the fictional narrative (a made-up story) "The Treasure Box" is read aloud.

The Treasure Box

Grandmother was a kind woman. She liked to buy presents for Sarah. Sarah was her only granddaughter. Grandmother always brought a white shopping bag to Sarah's house. The white bag held a gift for Sarah. The gift was always perfect.

When Grandmother arrived, she hugged Sarah. She hugged Sarah so tight Sarah could hardly breathe. Sarah looked at the bag. Grandmother smiled and said, "This is for you, my little girl." Grandmother reached into the bag. She pulled out a brown square box.

Sarah took the brown box from her grandmother's hand. The box was covered with small blue and red flowers. Sarah opened it slowly. It was empty.

"This is your treasure box, my little girl. Put your favorite things in the box to keep forever."

The next time Grandmother visited, Sarah was excited to show her the box. Inside the box was a hat covered in small flowers.

"Do you remember this hat?" asked Sarah. "You gave it to me last year. I put my special hat in my special box."

Sarah's grandmother smiled and gave her special granddaughter a big hug.

Step **2** Remember, a good fictional narrative (a made-up story) has the following parts.

- a title
- a character or characters you can picture in your mind
- a problem
- a beginning, a middle, and an end

Step **3** Use the following idea to plan your fictional narrative (a made-up story).

> **Write a story about a little boy or a little girl who found something. Write the story from your imagination.**

Step **4** Answer the planning questions to get ideas for your made-up story. Use your picture board or graphic organizer to help you think through your fictional narrative (a made-up story). You can use pictures or words to plan your fictional narrative (a made-up story).

FICTIONAL NARRATIVE

Planning Questions for a Made-Up Story

Use pictures or words.

Who are the characters?

Where does the story take place?

When does the story happen?

What happens in the story?

How does the story end?

FICTIONAL NARRATIVE

Picture Board for a Made-Up Story

Beginning:

Middle:

End:

FICTIONAL NARRATIVE

Graphic Organizer for a Made-Up Story

Title: _____

Beginning:

Middle:

End:

Write your fictional narrative (a made-up story).

Writing Activity 2

Step

5

_____

- -

_____

- -

_____

- -

_____

- -

_____

- -

_____

- -

_____

- -

_____

- -

_____

- -

_____

- -

_____

- -

If you need more room, ask a parent or a teacher for another piece of paper.

Step
6

The checklist shows what your best paper must have. Use the checklist below to review your work.

Checklist for Writing Activity 2

❏   My story has a title.

❏   My story is a made-up story.

❏   My characters have names.

❏   My story has a beginning, a middle, and an end.

❏   I try to spell words correctly.

❏   My sentences end with a period, an exclamation point, or a question mark.

❏   My sentences begin with capital letters.

Writing Activity 3: Personal Experience Narrative (A Story About Me)

Step 1 Follow along as the personal experience narrative (a story about me) "Leaves" is read aloud.

Leaves

My father decided it was time to rake the fall leaves. We walked into the yard. He handed me a rake that was just my size. I raked and raked the leaves. Slowly, a pile formed. The pile looked soft and inviting. I stepped away from the leaves and dropped the rake.

"Here I come, ready or not!" I took a running start and jumped into the pile of golden leaves. The leaves crunched as I jumped on them. My father laughed as the leaves scattered across the yard.

Dad helped me rake the leaves again. On my last jump, I heard a sound coming from behind the maple tree. "Meow!" A small kitten crawled toward the leaf pile. The kitten and the leaves were the same golden color. When the kitten came closer to the pile, I petted its soft fur.

"Dad! Dad! Look what I found!"

"Well, it looks like we have a new kitten," said Dad.

I took my new friend into the house. I put an old towel in a box to make a bed for the kitten. Mostly, she liked to stay in my lap. She purred and purred.

Later that night, my family thought of a perfect name for my new furry friend. We called our new pet "Leaves."

Step
2

Remember, a good personal experience narrative (a story about me) has the following parts.

- a title
- people you know
- a beginning, a middle, and an end

Step
3

Use the following idea to plan your personal experience narrative (a story about me).

> **Write about something that happened to you that was very funny. It could be something that happened at home, at school, or anywhere else.**

Step
4

Answer the planning questions to get ideas for your story about you. Use your picture board or graphic organizer to help you think through your personal experience narrative (a story about me). You can use pictures or words to plan your personal experience narrative (a story about me).

PERSONAL EXPERIENCE NARRATIVE

Planning Questions for a Story About Me

Use pictures or words.

Who was there?

What happened?

Where did it happen?

When did it happen?

What happened at the end?

PERSONAL EXPERIENCE NARRATIVE

Picture Board for a Story About Me

Beginning:

Middle:

End:

PERSONAL EXPERIENCE NARRATIVE

Graphic Organizer for a Story About Me

Title: _____

Beginning:

Middle:

End:

Write your personal experience narrative (a story about me).

Writing Activity 3

Step

5

If you need more room, ask a parent or a teacher for another piece of paper.

Step
6

The checklist shows what your best paper must have. Use the checklist below to review your work.

Checklist for Writing Activity 3

❑ My story has a title.

❑ My story is about me.

❑ My story has a beginning, a middle, and an end.

❑ I try to spell words correctly.

❑ I use interesting words.

❑ My sentences end with a period, an exclamation point, or a question mark.

❑ My sentences begin with a capital letter.

❑ Proper names begin with capital letters.

Writing Activity 4: Personal Experience Narrative (A Story About Me)

Step **1** Follow along as the personal experience narrative (a story about me) "The Spooky House" is read aloud.

The Spooky House

When I was five years old, I went to the State Fair. A very scary thing happened to me that day.

After hours of fun with my best friend, something caught my eye. The door to the "Spooky House" stood in front of me. My best friend stood by my side. I felt very brave. If we could go through the "Spooky House" together, I knew I would not be scared. Just as we reached the door, my friend ran to her parents. There I was, entering the dark "Spooky House" without my friend.

When I stepped through the door, I could not see anything. The room was very dark. There was no light. Creepy music was playing. After I took a few steps, a light flashed. I saw a mummy and a ghost. The scene scared me, so I started walking a little faster. I wanted to get away from those two.

As I made my way through the "Spooky House," all I could think about was seeing daylight. Each time a light flashed, I closed my eyes. I didn't want to see any more mummies or ghosts.

Finally, I came to the back door of the "Spooky House." When the sunlight hit my eyes, I saw my friend and her parents. Even though I had been scared, it felt good to go through the house by myself.

by Alexandra Grizinski

Step
2

Remember, a good personal experience narrative (a story about me) has the following parts.

- a title
- people you know
- a beginning, a middle, and an end

Step
3

Use the following idea to plan your personal experience narrative (a story about me).

> **Write about something that has happened to you. Write your personal experience narrative or story about me as if you were telling the story to a friend or a family member.**

Step
4

Answer the planning questions to get ideas for your story about you. Use your picture board or graphic organizer to help you think through your personal experience narrative (a story about me). You can use pictures or words to plan your personal experience narrative (a story about me).

PERSONAL EXPERIENCE NARRATIVE

Planning Questions for a Story About Me

Use pictures or words.

Who was there?

What happened?

Where did it happen?

When did it happen?

What happened at the end?

PERSONAL EXPERIENCE NARRATIVE

Picture Board for a Story About Me

Beginning:

Middle:

End:

PERSONAL EXPERIENCE NARRATIVE

Graphic Organizer for a Story About Me

Title: _____

Beginning:

Middle:

End:

Write your personal experience narrative (a story about me).

Writing Activity 4

Step

5

If you need more room, ask a parent or a teacher for another piece of paper.

Step
6

The checklist shows what your best paper must have. Use the checklist below to review your work.

Checklist for Writing Activity 4

❏ My story has a title.

❏ My story is about me.

❏ My story has a beginning, a middle, and an end.

❏ I try to spell words correctly.

❏ I use interesting words.

❏ My sentences end with a period, an exclamation point, or a question mark.

❏ My sentences begin with a capital letter.

❏ Proper names begin with capital letters.

Writing Activity 5: Retelling
(A Story I Retell in My Own Words)

Step
1

Follow along as two passages are read. The first passage is a story titled "Butterfly Tummy." The second passage is a retelling (a story I retell in my own words) of "Butterfly Tummy."

Butterfly Tummy

It was an early morning for Andy. He put on his slippers and walked quickly to the kitchen. Today was the big day. Today was Andy's first day at his new school. Andy's mother gave him a bowl of warm oatmeal. There was a little bit of brown sugar on top. Andy stirred his oatmeal. He could only eat half.

Andy felt a little tickle in his stomach. "You're nervous about school," his mom told him. "You have butterflies in your stomach." As he got dressed, he thought about his butterflies. A few minutes later, Andy heard the rumble of the yellow school bus. He grabbed his Mighty Hedgehog lunchbox and ran out the door. He still felt the tickle.

The bus pulled up to the big brick school. Mrs. Hartland greeted Andy as he stepped off the bus. She took his hand and led him to Room 108. The room was full of wonderful sights. Posters hung on the walls. A large carpet filled one corner, and there were books all around. Andy hoped one of the books was about Mighty Hedgehog, his favorite superhero.

"We keep something special over here," said Mrs. Hartland. A glass cage with a net over it sat by the window. Inside the glass cage, five orange and black Monarch butterflies fluttered about. Andy smiled.

"The classroom has butterflies, too," he thought to himself.

Step
1
continued

Retelling of "Butterfly Tummy"

Andy woke up early in the morning. It was his first day of school. He ate half a bowl of oatmeal for breakfast. He felt a tickle in his stomach. His mom told him he had butterflies. He rode the bus to school. He took his lunchbox with him. Mrs. Hartland met Andy when he got off the bus. She took him to his classroom. There was a cage in the classroom. It had butterflies in it. Andy smiled because he and the classroom both had butterflies.

Step
2

Remember, a good retelling (a story I retell in my own words) has the following parts.

- the title of the story
- my own words
- details from the story

Step
3

Use the following idea to plan your retelling (a story I retell in my own words).

Read the story titled "Soupy Sings at Sea" on page 32. Retell the story so the reader will know all the important facts of the story.

Step

3

continued

Soupy Sings at Sea

Soupy the Singing Seal liked to play in the ocean and spend time with her friends. Every afternoon, Soupy would sing for anyone who would listen. Soupy did not have a pretty voice, but she loved to sing.

One morning, Soupy dove into the water. She was looking for some food. Her brown body moved easily through the salt water. She swam to the ocean floor. She spotted a group of lobsters. Soupy loved to tease the lobsters. They had funny-looking claws and flat tails. Soupy kicked up sand. It swirled in the water. This made it hard for the lobsters to see. Soupy laughed and laughed.

"Why are you always picking on us?" asked Larry the Lobster. Soupy did not have an answer. "If you promise to stop picking on us, I will give you something special," Larry said.

"What can an ugly lobster give to a pretty seal?" Soupy wanted to know.

"You may be pretty, but your voice is not. I can teach you how to sing."

Soupy realized it did not feel good to be picked on. "I promise I will not pick on lobsters ever again," she said. "When can we start my singing lessons?"

Step

4

Answer the planning questions for the story you retell in your own words. Use your picture board or graphic organizer to help you think through your retelling (a story I retell in my own words). You can use pictures or words to plan your retelling (a story I retell in my own words).

RETELLING
Planning Questions for a Story I Retell in My Own Words

Title of the Story:

Who are the characters in the story?

Where does the story take place?

When does the story take place?

What happens at the end?

RETELLING
Picture Board for a Story I Retell in My Own Words

Beginning:

Middle:

End:

RETELLING
Graphic Organizer for a Story I Retell in My Own Words

Retell the Story in Order

Beginning:

Middle:

End:

Write your retelling (a story I retell in my own words).

Writing Activity 5

Step

5

_____

_____

_____

_____

_____

_____

_____

_____

_____

_____

_____

_____

_____

If you need more room, ask a parent or a teacher for another piece of paper.

Step
6

The checklist shows what your best paper must have. Use the checklist below to review your work.

Checklist for Writing Activity 5

❑ My retelling starts with the beginning of the story.

❑ I use my own words to retell the story.

❑ My retelling includes the beginning, the middle, and the end.

❑ I use details from the story.

❑ My sentences end with a period, an exclamation point, or a question mark.

❑ My sentences begin with capital letters.

Writing Activity 6: Retelling
(A Story I Retell in My Own Words)

Step
1

Follow along as two passages are read. The first passage is a story titled "Rainy Day Picnic." The second passage is a retelling (a story I retell in my own words) of "Rainy Day Picnic."

Rainy Day Picnic

Jamie had looked forward to this Saturday all week. His father said it was going to be Picnic Day. Jamie was sad when he looked out the window on Saturday morning. Rain was pouring from the sky. The clouds were dark. The trees moved with the blowing winds. "So much for Picnic Day," Jamie thought to himself.

In the kitchen, Jamie was surprised to find his dad packing the picnic basket. The table was covered with some of the family's favorite foods. Apples, cookies, peanut butter sandwiches, and pretzels were wrapped in plastic bags. Four juice boxes, napkins, and plates were also on the table.

"Where are we going on a rainy day?" Jamie asked.

"It's a surprise," said his dad. He finished packing the basket and closed the lid. "I know you will love it. Let's get going." When the family got in the car, Jamie's dad told him to close his eyes and keep them closed until he said, "We're here."

The family drove for a few minutes. Then, Jamie's dad stopped the car. "We're here," he said. Jamie opened his eyes. The car was parked in their own driveway. Everyone laughed. "I'm not letting rain ruin our Picnic Day," said Jamie's dad.

The family went inside. They spread a blanket on the floor. They ate the picnic lunch. Jamie's family told jokes and read books. Even though it was raining, everyone had a good time.

Step

1

continued

Retelling of "Rainy Day Picnic"

Jamie woke up on Saturday. It was raining. He was sad because his family was supposed to go on a picnic. When Jamie went to the kitchen, he found his dad packing the picnic basket. All the family's favorite foods were on the table. Jamie's dad said they were going on the picnic, even though it was raining. They got in the car, and Jamie closed his eyes until the family got to the picnic place. When Jamie opened his eyes, they were at his house. The family had the picnic on a blanket in the house. They ate, shared stories, and had a good time.

Step

2

Remember, a good retelling (a story I retell in my own words) has the following parts.

- the title of the story
- my own words
- details from the story

Step

3

Use the following idea to plan your retelling (a story I retell in my own words).

Read the story titled "Hendrik's Mountain Adventure" on page 40. Retell the story so the reader will know all the important facts of the story.

Step

3
continued

Hendrik's Mountain Adventure

In the mountains of a faraway place, there stands a sleepy little village called Vestorlennordland. The mountains are steep, and there are very few people who can find their way to the village. Of those who make the trip, almost none can say the name.

Hendrik Arvid is a young boy who lives in Vestorlennordland. His dream is to see the world outside the village. He plans and plans, and one day, he decides to start traveling. He packs a lunch of fish, yogurt, and cheese. After putting on a warm coat, he and his goat, Olaf, start their trip.

He walks down the mountain. He meets Mr. Gudrun. Mr. Gudrun is a woodcutter. "I'm going to see the world outside my village," Hendrik tells the woodcutter. Mr. Gudrun wishes Hendrik luck, and Hendrik keeps walking.

Hendrik walks up another mountain. He sees Mrs. Inger. She is gathering wild flowers. "I want to see the world," he tells her. She smiles and gives Olaf a pat on the head. Hendrik feels a little sad as he gets farther from his village.

Hendrik reaches a third mountain. Mr. Jorun is driving toward the village. "Where are you heading?" he asks Hendrik.

"Can you take me and Olaf back to the village?" asks Hendrik. He is happy when Mr. Jorun agrees. Although he wants to see distant places, he is most happy when he sees his own home.

Step

4

Answer the planning questions for the story you retell in your own words. Use your picture board or graphic organizer to help you think through your retelling (a story I retell in my own words). You can use pictures or words to plan your retelling (a story I retell in my own words).

RETELLING
Planning Questions for a Story I Retell in My Own Words

Title of the Story:

Who are the characters in the story?

Where does the story take place?

When does the story take place?

What happens at the end?

RETELLING
Picture Board for a Story I Retell in My Own Words

Beginning:

Middle:

End:

RETELLING

**Graphic Organizer for a Story I
Retell in My Own Words**

Retell the Story in Order

Beginning:

Middle:

End:

Write your retelling (a story I retell in my own words).

Writing Activity 6

Step 5

If you need more room, ask a parent or a teacher for another piece of paper.

Step

6

The checklist shows what your best paper must have. Use the checklist below to review your work.

Checklist for Writing Activity 6

❑ My retelling starts with the beginning of the story.

❑ I use my own words to retell the story.

❑ My retelling includes the beginning, the middle, and the end.

❑ I use details from the story.

❑ My sentences end with a period, an exclamation point, or a question mark.

❑ My sentences begin with capital letters.

Chapter 2

Description
(Journal and Letter)

What is Description?

The purpose of description is to create a picture. You should write descriptions when you want to let readers know how something looks, feels, sounds, tastes, or smells.

A **journal** is like a diary. You can record your thoughts and ideas in journals. Some things you may write about in journals include: memories, hobbies, pets, friends, family, and vacations.

A **letter** includes a date, a greeting, a body, a closing, and a signature. When you write a letter, you are writing to a particular person or group.

Writing Activity 7:
A Descriptive Journal

Step
1
Follow along as the December 10, 2002 journal entry is read.

December 10, 2002
Journal Entry

Today, I spent some time with Grandma. When I woke up, it was cold and dark outside. It was Saturday. I was happy because I did not have to go to school. I stayed in my pajamas. I sat on the couch and watched early morning cartoons. Mom had to go to work, so Grandma came to my house to stay with me. She gave me a hug and sat down on the couch to watch cartoons with me.

At noon, she made my favorite lunch. She carefully poured macaroni and cheese into two bowls. We sat together. We talked and laughed as we ate our tasty lunch. Later, we turned off the TV. We snuggled in Dad's chair. She read a book to me. What a great day! I am so lucky to have such a loving grandmother. She makes every visit special.

Step

2

Remember, a good journal entry has the following parts.

- a date
- a description of the day
- a description of your feelings
- a beginning, a middle, and an end

Step

3

Use the following idea to plan your journal entry.

> **Think about the part of your day that you like best. Date your journal and write about the best part of your day.**

Step

4

Answer the planning questions to get ideas for your journal. Use your picture board or graphic organizer to help you think through your journal entry. You can use pictures or words to plan your journal entry.

JOURNAL ENTRY

Planning Questions for a Journal Entry

Use pictures or words.

Why are you writing about this day or time?

Who was there?

Where did it happen?

When did it happen?

What happened?

How did you feel?

JOURNAL ENTRY

Picture Board for a Journal Entry

Date:

Beginning:

Middle:

End:

How did you feel?

JOURNAL ENTRY

Graphic Organizer for a Journal Entry

Date:

What Happened?

Beginning:

Middle:

End:

How did you feel?

Write your journal entry.

Writing Activity 7

Step
5

_____

- -

_____

- -

_____

- -

_____

- -

_____

- -

_____

- -

_____

- -

_____

- -

_____

- -

_____

If you need more room, ask a parent or a teacher for another piece of paper.

Step

6

The checklist shows what your best paper must have. Use the checklist below to review your work.

Checklist for Writing Activity 7

❑ My journal entry has a date.

❑ I describe people, places, things, and events from my day to make a picture.

❑ My journal entry has a beginning, a middle, and an end.

❑ I use words that tell what I heard, saw, and felt.

❑ My sentences end with a period, an exclamation point, or a question mark.

❑ My sentences begin with capital letters.

Writing Activity 8:
A Descriptive Journal

Step Follow along as the July 4, 2002 journal entry is read.

1

July 4, 2002
Journal Entry

What a great day this has been! I have gone to parades before, but this Fourth of July parade was the best. My brother and I stood on the side of Main Street. We ate ice cream and waited for the parade to begin.

The parade started with a group of clowns. The clowns were dressed in brightly-colored outfits. They threw candy and passed out balloons. Next, a group of horses trotted down the street. They had shiny black coats. There were ribbons in their manes. A big red firetruck rolled behind the horses. The firefighters waved. When I heard a drumroll, I knew the marching band was coming. As they moved past me and my brother, the horns blew and the music started. The band was loud! There were many other sights, but I was most proud when I saw my uncle in the parade. He wore his policeman's uniform. He carried an American flag. I was very proud of him. I wanted everyone to know he was my uncle. He made the parade very special.

Step

2

Remember, a good journal entry has the following parts.

- a date
- a description of the day
- a description of your feelings
- a beginning, a middle, and an end

Step

3

Use the following idea to plan your journal entry.

Think about a time you spent with a person or a pet you love. Describe what the person or the pet looks like, sounds like, and how the person or pet makes you feel.

Step

4

Answer the planning questions to get ideas for your journal. Use your picture board or graphic organizer to help you think through your journal entry. You can use pictures or words to plan your journal entry.

JOURNAL ENTRY

Planning Questions for a Journal Entry

Use pictures or words.

Why are you writing about this day or time?

Who was there?

Where did it happen?

When did it happen?

What happened?

How did you feel?

JOURNAL ENTRY

Picture Board for a Journal Entry

Date:

Beginning:

Middle:

End:

How did you feel?

JOURNAL ENTRY

Graphic Organizer for a Journal Entry

Date:

What Happened?

Beginning:

Middle:

End:

How did you feel?

Write your journal entry.

Writing Activity 8

Step
5

_____

If you need more room, ask a parent or a teacher for another piece of paper.

Step
6

The checklist shows what your best paper must have. Use the checklist below to review your work.

Checklist for Writing Activity 8

❑   My journal entry has a date.

❑   I describe people, places, things, and events from my day to make a picture.

❑   My journal entry has a beginning, a middle, and an end.

❑   I use words that tell what I heard, saw, and felt.

❑   My sentences end with a period, an exclamation point, or a question mark.

❑   My sentences begin with capital letters.

Writing Activity 9:
A Descriptive Letter

Step Follow along as the descriptive letter is read aloud.

1

From Bill's Desk

March 16, 2002

Dear Bob,

   I am glad you are here. I am writing to welcome you to the neighborhood. I heard your family just moved in. Mrs. Robinson told me she thinks you are about my age. I am seven.

   Let me tell you about myself. I am in first grade. I go to Eastgate Elementary School. I like to play outside when the weather is warm. I really like to ride my bike. Sometimes, on summer evenings, the kids in the neighborhood catch lightning bugs. We put them in jars. I usually let mine go after an hour or so. Maybe you can join us sometime.

   I hope we can meet soon. Write back and tell me about yourself.

Sincerely,

Bill

Step
2

Remember, a good descriptive letter has the following parts.

- a date
- a greeting
- a body that talks to the reader
- a closing
- a signature

Step
3

Use the following idea to plan your descriptive letter.

> **Write a friendly letter to someone in your class. Write to someone who doesn't know you very well. Describe yourself so the reader knows who you are. Maybe the reader will want to meet you after reading your letter.**

Step
4

Use the planning guide to get ideas for your letter. Use your graphic organizer to help you think through your descriptive letter. You can use pictures or words to plan your descriptive letter.

DESCRIPTIVE LETTER

Planning Guide for a Descriptive Letter

Date

Month, Day, Year

Greeting

Dear (Capitalized Name),

Body

Beginning

Greet the reader:

- I hope you are . . .
- I am writing to you because . . .

Middle

Tell about something you did.
Tell about something that happened.
Tell something about you.

End

Closing comment:

- Hope to hear from you soon.
- Write back to me.

Closing

Your nephew,
Your niece,
Your grandson,
Your granddaughter,
Your friend,
Sincerely,
Love,

Signature

(Your Name)

DESCRIPTIVE LETTER

Graphic Organizer for a Descriptive Letter

Date:

Greeting:

Why you are writing:

Body:

Personal comments ending the letter:

Closing:

Signature:

Write your descriptive letter.

Writing Activity 9

Step

5

If you need more room, ask a parent or a teacher for another piece of paper.

Step
6
The checklist shows what your best paper must have. Use the checklist below to review your work.

Checklist for Writing Activity 9

❑ I use the form for a letter, including:
- a date,
- a greeting,
- a body,
- a closing, and
- a signature.

❑ My letter tells my reader why I am writing and makes personal comments.

❑ I use words that help the reader:
- hear,
- see,
- feel, and
- think.

❑ My letter includes a personal closing comment.

❑ My sentences end with a period, an exclamation point, or a question mark.

❑ My sentences begin with capital letters.

Writing Activity 10:
A Descriptive Letter

Step Follow along as the descriptive letter is read aloud.

1

September 20, 2002

Dear Brandon,

I hope you are fine. I wanted to write you to let you know my new address. It is 8567 Woodview Drive. We just moved into our new house. I have my own room. My sister has her own room, too. There is plenty of room for me, my toys, and my two gerbils. I named one of the gerbils after you.

My new backyard has room for the swing set. This yard has a fence. Buddy runs and runs until he is so tired he cannot run anymore. My dad said he is going to plant a vegetable garden in one corner. It is a spot that gets a lot of sunlight. I hope I do not have to eat more vegetables. Even with the garden, there will be plenty of room to play soccer.

I have made a few new friends, but I miss everyone from our old neighborhood. I hope your mom will let you visit me soon. Write to me and tell me what is happening with you.

Your friend,

Brent

Step
2

Remember, a good descriptive letter has the following parts.

- a date
- a greeting
- a body that talks to the reader
- a closing
- a signature

Step
3

Use the following idea to plan your descriptive letter.

> **Write a friendly letter to a new pen pal. Describe your classroom. Use words that will help your pen pal see the classroom as you see it.**

Step
4

Use the planning guide to get ideas for your letter. Use your graphic organizer to help you think through your descriptive letter. You can use pictures or words to plan your descriptive letter.

DESCRIPTIVE LETTER

Planning Guide for a Descriptive Letter

Date

Month, Day, Year

Greeting

Dear (Capitalized Name),

Body

Beginning

Greet the reader:

- I hope you are . . .
- I am writing to you because . . .

Middle

Tell about something you did.
Tell about something that happened.
Tell something about you.

End

Closing comment:

- Hope to hear from you soon.
- Write back to me.

Closing

Your nephew,
Your niece,
Your grandson,
Your granddaughter,
Your friend,
Sincerely,
Love,

Signature

(Your Name)

DESCRIPTIVE LETTER

Graphic Organizer for a Descriptive Letter

Date:

Greeting:

Why you are writing:

Body:

Personal comments ending the letter:

Closing:

Signature:

Write your descriptive letter.

Writing Activity 10

Step

5

_____

- -

_____

- -

_____

- -

_____

- -

_____

- -

_____

- -

_____

- -

_____

- -

_____

- -

_____

- -

_____

- -

_____

If you need more room, ask a parent or a teacher for another piece of paper.

Step
6

The checklist shows what your best paper must have. Use the checklist below to review your work.

Checklist for Writing Activity 10

❑ I use the form for a letter, including:
- a date,
- a greeting,
- a body,
- a closing, and
- a signature.

❑ My letter tells my reader why I am writing and makes personal comments.

❑ I use words that help the reader:
- hear,
- see,
- feel, and
- think.

❑ My letter includes a personal closing comment.

❑ My sentences end with a period, an exclamation point, or a question mark.

❑ My sentences begin with capital letters.

Chapter 3

Directions
(Directions and Invitation)

What are Directions?

The purpose of directions is to tell someone how to make something or do something.

Directions

- can tell the reader how to make something, like a recipe.
- can tell the reader how to go somewhere, like a map.
- should be in step-by-step order.
- should be easy for the reader to follow.

An **invitation** is a short note or a letter that invites someone to an event such as a birthday party. Invitations include:

- what the event is,
- where the event is,
- the time of the event,
- the date of the event, and
- an RSVP (to tell them if you can come).

Writing Activity 11: Directions
(How to Do Something)

Step
1

Follow along as the directions on how to fix a bowl of cereal are read aloud.

How to Fix a Bowl of Cereal

To fix a bowl of cereal, you need a box of cereal, a bowl, a spoon, and some milk. First, pick the type of cereal you like to eat. Second, open the cereal box. Next, pour the cereal into a bowl. Then, open the milk container. Carefully pour the milk over the cereal. Don't pour too much milk into the bowl. If the bowl gets too full, the cereal will spill out. Finally, get your spoon and start to eat. You now know how to fix a bowl of cereal, so crunch away and enjoy your cereal.

Step

2

Remember, good directions have the following parts.

- a beginning that tells the reader what the directions will explain how to do
- a description of what is needed to complete the task
- steps that are given in order
- a starting point and an ending point

Step

3

Use the following idea to plan your directions.

Your friend loves chocolate milk but has never made it. Write directions for your friend. After reading your directions, your friend should be able to make chocolate milk.

Step

4

Use the planning guide to get ideas for your directions. Use your graphic organizer to help you think through your directions. You can use pictures or words to plan your directions.

DIRECTIONS

Planning Guide for How To Do Something

How To: _____

WORDS YOU COULD USE IN YOUR DIRECTIONS:

Order words

first	second	third
next	then	finally

Prepositions

in	under	after	behind
on	before	over	beneath
around	next to	near	

Doing verbs

mix	stir	pour
blend	insert	

Sentence starters

First, you will . . .
Then, you should . . .
Finally, you will . . .

DIRECTIONS

Graphic Organizer for How To Do Something

How To: _____

What You Need to Begin:

Steps to Follow:

1.

2.

3.

Ending Comment:

Write your directions.

Writing Activity 11

Step

5

_____

If you need more room, ask a parent or a teacher for another piece of paper.

Step **6** The checklist shows what your best paper must have. Use the checklist below to review your work.

Checklist for Writing Activity 11

❑ My directions begin with a sentence that tells what my directions will explain how to do.

❑ I tell what materials are needed to begin the task.

❑ I use the correct order to tell the reader what steps to follow.

❑ I include an ending comment describing the completed task.

❑ My sentences end with a period, an exclamation point, or a question mark.

❑ My sentences begin with capital letters.

Writing Activity 12: Directions
(How to Go Somewhere)

Step 1 Look at the picture below. Follow along in your booklets now as the set of directions on how to get to the toy section of the store are read aloud.

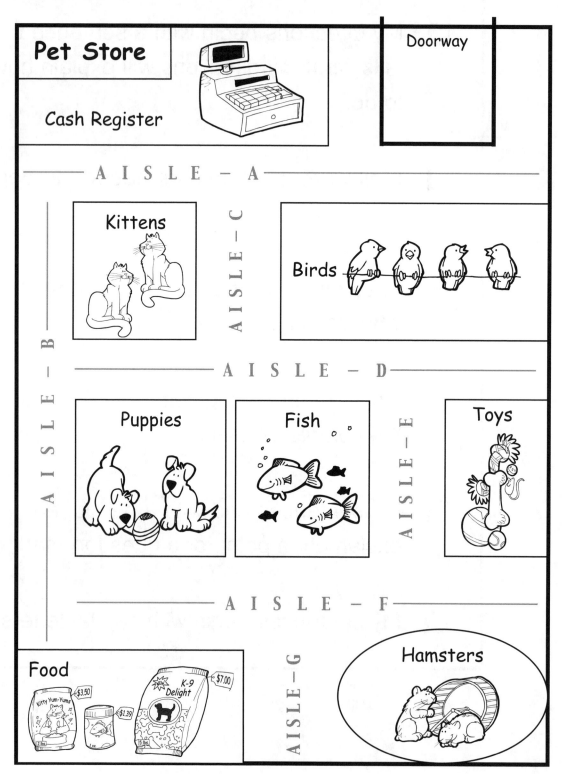

Step

1

continued

When you give directions, you have to picture yourself facing the direction you want to go as you follow the steps.

Your friend wants to buy a toy for a new pet. Turn the pet store map and pretend you are entering the door. Give your friend directions to the toy section.

1. When you walk into the store, you will see the cash register on your right and the birds in front of you.

2. Turn right and walk down Aisle A.

3. When you see the kittens, turn left and walk down Aisle C.

4. When you see the puppies and the fish in front of you, turn left and walk down Aisle D.

5. Go to the end of Aisle D and the toys will be on your right.

6. Select the toy your friend's pet will enjoy the most!

* Note: There is more than one way to give directions to the toy section.

Step

2

Remember, good directions have the following parts.

- a beginning that tells the reader what the directions will explain how to do
- a description of what is needed to complete the task
- steps that are given in order
- a starting point and an ending point

Step

3

Use the following idea to plan your directions.

Your friend is in aisle E and is looking at the toys. Write directions for your friend. Tell your friend how to get from the toy section to the door.

Step

3
continued

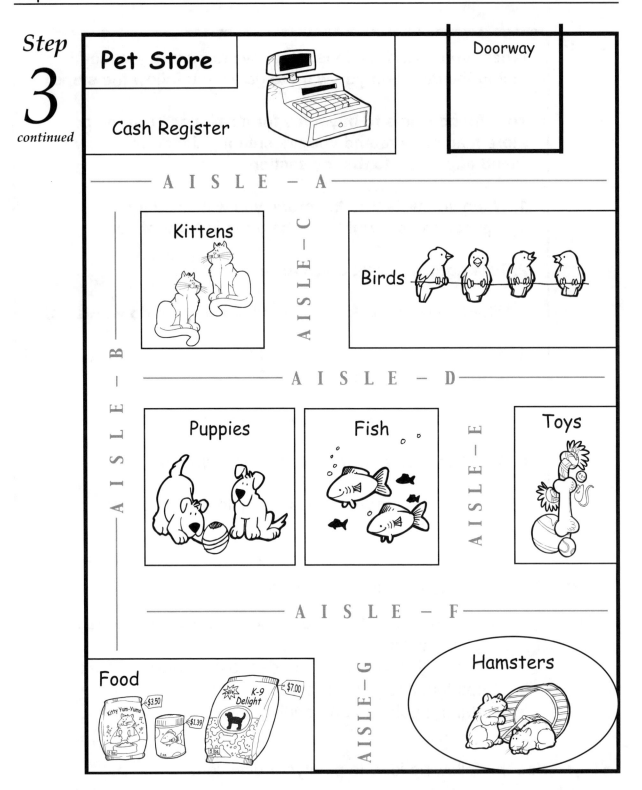

Step

4

Use your planning guide to get ideas for your directions. Use your graphic organizer to help you think through your directions. You can use pictures or words to plan your directions.

DIRECTIONS

Planning Guide for How To Go Somewhere

How To: _____

WORDS YOU COULD USE IN YOUR DIRECTIONS:

Order words

first	second	third
next	then	finally

Prepositions

in	under	after	behind
on	before	over	beneath
around	next to	near	toward

Direction words

north	south	left
east	west	right

Sentence starters

	Before you get to. . .
First, you will . . .	At the stop sign . . .
Then, you should . . .	At the light . . .
Finally, you will . . .	At the intersection . . .
When you see . . .	At the corner . . .

DIRECTIONS

Graphic Organizer for How To Go Somewhere

How To: _____

Where you are going:

Where to start:

Steps to Follow:

1.

2.

3.

Where you will end up:

Write your directions.

Writing Activity 12

Step **5**

If you need more room, ask a parent or a teacher for another piece of paper.

Step

6

The checklist shows what your best paper must have. Use the checklist below to review your work.

Checklist for Writing Activity 12

❑ My directions begin with a sentence that tells where my directions will take the reader.

❑ I tell where to start.

❑ I give the directions in the correct order to get to the location.

❑ I include an ending comment telling where the reader will end.

❑ My sentences end with a period, an exclamation point, or a question mark.

❑ My sentences begin with capital letters.

Writing Activity 13:
Invitation

Step Follow along as the invitation is read aloud.

1

September 25, 2002

Dear Bart,

My birthday is almost here, and I'm having a party. You are invited to come to my birthday party on October 12, 2002. I live at 6298 Brownstone Court. The party will begin at 2:00 p.m. It will end at 4:00 p.m. We will play games and eat cake. We will have lots of fun. Call 555-5555 by October 5th to let me know if you can come. I hope to see you there.

Sincerely,

Lori

Step
2

Remember, a good invitation has the following parts.

- information about where and when to attend
- the purpose of the event
- information for an RSVP
- all important details about the event

Step
3

Use the following idea to plan your invitation.

You are going to have a party. Write an invitation to your friends so they will know why you are having the party.

Step
4

Use your planning guide to get ideas for your invitation. Use your graphic organizer to help you think through your invitation. You can use pictures or words to plan your invitation.

INVITATION

Planning Guide for an Invitation

Date
- Month, Day, Year

Who is invited? Dear
- name of person who can come
- name of group who can come

What is the invitation for?
- birthday party
- sports team party
- Scouts' party
- classroom event
- special event

When?
- date the party or event will occur

Where? (location)
- include a map
- include an address

Other important information
- what will happen at the event
- what to bring or to wear

RSVP to whom?
- name and telephone number for the guests to call to tell if they can come

RSVP when?
- what date guests need to call by to tell if they can come

Closing
- Sincerely
- Your classmate
- Your friend

Signature
- Team Name
- Your Name
- Class Name

INVITATION

Graphic Organizer for an Invitation

Date

Who is invited?

What is the invitation for?

When?

Where?

Other important information

RSVP to whom?

RSVP when?

Closing

Signature

Write your invitation.

Writing Activity 13

Step

5

If you need more room, ask a parent or a teacher for another piece of paper.

Step
6

The checklist shows what your best paper must have. Use the checklist below to review your work.

Checklist for Writing Activity 13

❑ My invitation includes all the important details for my guest, such as:

- what the invitation is for,
- when to attend,
- who is invited,
- RSVP information (for guests to tell if they can come), and
- a closing with a name or a signature.

❑ My sentences end with a period, an exclamation point, or a question mark.

❑ My sentences begin with capital letters.

Writing Activity 14:
Invitation

Step Follow along as the invitation is read aloud.

1

December 1, 2002

Dear Grandpa,

    I am writing to invite you to a holiday concert at my school. The concert will be held at New Hope Elementary School on December 20, 2002. The concert starts at 9:00 a.m. and ends at 10:00 a.m. After the concert, you are invited to stay for cookies and punch. We will be singing many holiday songs. You are welcome to sing along, if you would like. I would really like to see you there. I hope you can make it. Please check your calendar and RSVP by December 13th by calling 333-3333.

Love,

Blake

Step
2

Remember, a good invitation has the following parts.

- information about where and when to attend
- the purpose of the event
- information for an RSVP
- all important details about the event

Step
3

Use the following idea to plan your invitation.

> **Your class is having a party for people who volunteer in your classroom. Write an invitation. Invite the volunteers to this special party.**

Step
4

Use your planning guide to get ideas for your invitation. Use your graphic organizer to help you think through your invitation. You can use pictures or words to plan your invitation.

INVITATION

Planning Guide for an Invitation

Date
- Month, Day, Year

Who is invited? Dear
- name of person who can come
- name of group who can come

What is the invitation for?
- birthday party
- Scouts' party
- special event
- sports team party
- classroom event

When?
- date the party or event will occur

Where? (location)
- include a map
- include an address

Other important information
- what will happen at the event
- what to bring or to wear

RSVP to whom?
- telephone number for the guests to call to tell if they can come

RSVP when?
- what date guests need to call by to tell if they can come

Closing
- Sincerely
- Your friend
- Your classmate

Signature
- Team Name
- Your Name
- Class Name

INVITATION

Graphic Organizer for an Invitation

Date

Who is invited?

What is the invitation for?

When?

Where?

Other important information

RSVP to whom?

RSVP when?

Closing

Signature

Write your invitation.

Writing Activity 14

Step 5

If you need more room, ask a parent or a teacher for another piece of paper.

Step
6

The checklist shows what your best paper must have. Use the checklist below to review your work.

Checklist for Writing Activity 14

❑ My invitation includes all the important details for my guest, such as:

- what the invitation is for,
- when to attend,
- who is invited,
- RSVP information (for guests to tell if they can come), and
- a closing with a name or a signature.

❑ My sentences end with a period, an exclamation point, or a question mark.

❑ My sentences begin with capital letters.

Chapter 4

Explanation
(Informational Report, Summary, and Thank-You Note)

What is Explanation?

Writers give an explanation when they want readers to understand something. An explanation uses facts or details.

An **informational report** contains facts. Reports can be written on real people, places, things, or events. An informational report is nonfiction.

A **summary** is short. A summary gives only the main ideas; it does not contain details. A summary should be written in your own words.

A **thank-you note** is a short note thanking someone for something that was given to you or done for you. A thank-you note is written in the form of a letter; it includes a date, a greeting, a body, a closing, and a signature.

Writing Activity 15:
Informational Report

Step Follow along as the informational report "Rabbits" is read aloud.

1

Rabbits

Rabbits are mammals. They have fur that is soft and thick. They have short, fuzzy tails and long ears. Rabbits use their strong back legs and feet to run and to hop.

Rabbits like to eat plants, flowers, grass, clover, and vegetables. Many times, rabbits will eat from people's gardens. This causes some people to think rabbits are pests.

Rabbits live near fields, shrubs, and grassy places. Rabbits make their homes in underground holes or in shrubs. These homes provide shelter.

You can see rabbits any time of day. However, rabbits are most active during the early evening and at night. Be careful; if you scare them, the only things you will see are their fuzzy tails as they dart away!

Next time you are outside, keep your eye out for these mammals. Are the rabbits you see cute creatures or harmful pests?

Step

2

Remember, an informational report has the following parts.

- a title
- a sentence telling what the report is about
- important information about the topic
- details about what I have learned about the topic
- a summary that ends the report

Step

3

Use the following idea to plan your informational report.

Read through the information given about emergency medical technicians on the next page. Use the planning questions on page 105 to gather information. Use the information you gather in the planning questions to complete your graphic organizer.

You do not have to use every fact to complete your informational report. You will need to organize the material and add words of your own.

Write an informational report about emergency medical technicians using the facts given. Use the graphic organizer to write an introduction, a paragraph, and a summary that ends your report.

Step

3

continued

Emergency Medical Technicians

- Emergency medical technicians are called EMTs.

- EMTs work in fire departments.

- EMTs take people to the hospital.

- EMTs put bandages on cuts.

- EMTs go to car crashes and fires.

- Gloves help EMTs stay safe and healthy.

- EMTs give medical care to people during an emergency.

- EMTs treat people who are sick.

- EMTs put splints on broken bones.

- EMTs help people who are hurt.

- EMTs give oxygen to people who cannot breathe.

- EMTs wear sterile gloves.

- EMTs save lives.

- EMTs drive ambulances.

- EMTs use backboards to carry people who are hurt.

Step

4

Use your planning questions and your graphic organizer to help you think through your informational report. You can use pictures or words to plan your informational report.

INFORMATIONAL REPORT

Planning Questions

Topic:

Planning Questions	Key Words – Short Notes
Who (or what) are they?	
What do they do?	
What do they look like?	
Where do they live?	
Why are they important?	
Summary: What are the most important things you have learned about this topic?	

INFORMATIONAL REPORT
Graphic Organizer

Title: _____

Introduction (What is the report about?)

Paragraph (What did you learn?)

Summary (What are the most important points?)

Write your informational report.

Writing Activity 15

Step 5

If you need more room, ask a parent or a teacher for another piece of paper.

Step
6

The checklist shows what your best paper must have. Use the checklist below to review your work.

Checklist for Writing Activity 15

❏ My informational report has a title.

❏ My informational report has a beginning that tells the reader what my report is about.

❏ My informational report has a paragraph that tells the reader what I have learned.

❏ My informational report includes a summary of the most important parts.

❏ My sentences end with a period, an exclamation point, or a question mark.

❏ My sentences begin with capital letters.

Writing Activity 16:
Informational Report

Step

1

Follow along as the informational report "Wind" is read aloud.

Wind

Wind is moving air. We cannot see wind, but we can see wind move things. We can see wind push clouds across the sky or rustle the leaves on trees. Wind can carry a kite high toward the sky. It can blow wind chimes, which make pretty sounds. Wind can move a sailboat across the water. Wind carries the seeds of plants to new places where they can take root and grow. These are good things about wind.

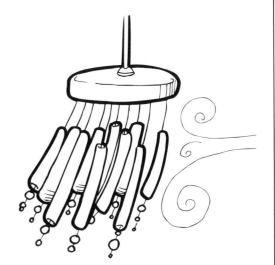

Sometimes, when wind is strong, it can cause damage. Strong wind can knock over trees and telephone poles. Strong wind can cause objects to fly through the air and break things. If the ground is dry, strong wind can blow away topsoil.

Wind can be gentle or strong. On warm days, wind causes air to move. This cools us down and feels good against our skin. Other times, wind can blow very hard. This type of wind can cause damage. Sometimes wind helps us, but sometimes it does not.

Step
2

Remember, an informational report has the following parts.

- a title
- a sentence telling what the report is about
- important information about the topic
- details about what I have learned about the topic
- a summary that ends the report

Step
3

Use the following idea to plan your informational report.

Read through the information given about wolves on the next page. Use the planning questions on page 112 to gather information. Use the information you gather in the planning questions to complete your graphic organizer.

You do not have to use every fact to complete your informational report. You will need to organize the material and add words of your own.

Write an informational report about wolves using the facts given. Use the graphic organizer to write an introduction, a paragraph, and a summary that ends your report.

Step

3

continued

Wolves

- Wolves live in many different places.
- A wolf is a type of wild dog.
- Each wolf pack has a leader.
- A group of wolves is called a pack.
- Wolves look for food and water together.
- A wolf can have as many as 11 pups at a time.
- Sometimes wolves live in dens.
- A baby wolf is called a pup.
- Wolves are like dogs.
- Wolves do many things in packs.
- Wolves hunt many kinds of animals.
- A den may be a cave or a hollow log.
- Wolves grow thick fur in the winter.
- The other wolves follow the leader of the pack.
- Wolves share their food with the pack.
- Wolf pups are born in the winter.
- Sometimes dens are underground.
- Wolves can bark, growl, and howl.
- The adult wolves take care of their young pups.
- Dogs are better pets than wolves.
- Wolves are wild animals.

Step

4

Use your planning questions and your graphic organizer to help you think through your informational report. You can use pictures or words to plan your informational report.

INFORMATIONAL REPORT
Planning Questions

Topic:

Planning Questions	Key Words – Short Notes
Who (or what) are they?	
What do they do?	
What do they look like?	
Where do they live?	
Why are they important?	
Summary: What are the most important things you have learned about this topic?	

INFORMATIONAL REPORT
Graphic Organizer

Title: _____

Introduction (What is the report about?)

Paragraph (What did you learn?)

Summary (What are the most important points?)

Write your informational report.

Writing Activity 16

Step

5

_____

If you need more room, ask a parent or a teacher for another piece of paper.

Step
6

The checklist shows what your best paper must have. Use the checklist below to review your work.

Checklist for Writing Activity 16

❑ My informational report has a title.

❑ My informational report has a beginning that tells the reader what my report is about.

❑ My informational report has a paragraph that tells the reader what I have learned.

❑ My informational report includes a summary of the most important parts.

❑ My sentences end with a period, an exclamation point, or a question mark.

❑ My sentences begin with capital letters.

Writing Activity 17: Summary
(Only the Main Ideas)

Step
1
Follow along as two passages are read aloud. The first passage is a report titled "George Washington Carver." The second passage is a summary of "George Washington Carver."

George Washington Carver

George Washington Carver was born in 1864 in Missouri. He lived and worked on the Moses Plantation until he was ten years old. His work on the plantation helped George develop his love of the outdoors and science. He left the plantation to move to another town so he could go to school.

George is best known for his work with peanuts. He developed over 300 uses for the peanut. He also developed many uses for soybeans, pecans, and sweet potatoes. You might recognize some of the things he helped develop. Some of the things he made using peanuts include buttermilk, chili sauce, glue, ink, instant coffee, laundry soap, mayonnaise, metal polish, paint, paper, plastic, shampoo, shaving cream, shoe polish, talcum powder, and wood stain.

As you can see, George Washington Carver's many inventions are important in our lives today. If it were not for his work, things might be very different. George was one of the greatest inventors of all time!

Step

1

continued

Summary of "George Washington Carver"

George Washington Carver was from Missouri. He was born in 1864. He lived on the Moses Plantation. He loved nature and science. He developed many uses for the peanut. He invented many things we still use today. George Washington Carver was a great inventor.

Step

2

Remember, a good summary (only the main ideas) has the following parts.

- main ideas
- no unimportant or unnecessary information
- a small amount of detail
- my own words

Step

3

Use the following idea to plan your summary (only the main ideas).

Read the report titled "Parrots" on page 118. Write a summary (only the main ideas).

Step
3
continued

Parrots

Parrots are brightly colored birds. They usually live in places where the weather is warm and wet. Many types of parrots have green feathers. Parrots with green feathers are the most common. Parrots can also have blue, yellow, red, purple, pink, brown, or black feathers.

Parrots have four toes. Two of their toes point forward. Two of their toes are turned backward. This makes them walk strangely, but they are great climbers. They use their toes and their bills to help them move from branch to branch.

Parrots eat mostly seeds and fruits. They like to build their nests in holes found in the ground, in trees, or in rocks.

Parrots are very smart. Some parrots make noises that sound like human voices. This is why some people like to have parrots as pets. There is one thing you should know: if you buy a parrot just to hear it talk, you might be unhappy. Only a small number of parrots ever learn to talk.

by Lainie Burke

Step
4
Use your planning guide and graphic organizer to help you think through your summary (only the main ideas). You can use pictures or words to plan your summary (only the main ideas).

STEPS FOR WRITING A SUMMARY

Planning Guide for Including Only the Main Ideas

Topic: _____

Complete the Following Steps:

Step 1   ❏ **Skim the reading selection and begin to look for the main idea.**

Step 2   ❏ **Underline the topic sentence for each paragraph in the text selection.** (If there is no topic sentence, write one for the paragraph.)

Step 3   ❏ **Cross out unimportant information in the text selection.**

Step 4   ❏ **Cross out information that is repeated.**

STEPS FOR WRITING A SUMMARY

Graphic Organizer Including Only the Main Ideas

Topic: _____

Write what the text selection is about. Include only important information.

Beginning:

Main Idea:

Ending:

Write your summary.

Writing Activity 17

Step

5

If you need more room, ask a parent or a teacher for another piece of paper.

Step
6

The checklist shows what your best paper must have. Use the checklist below to review your work.

Checklist for Writing Activity 17

❏ My summary includes only important information.

❏ My summary starts at the beginning.

❏ My summary states the main idea.

❏ My summary has an ending.

❏ My summary does not include information that is not important.

❏ My sentences end with a period, an exclamation point, or a question mark.

❏ My sentences begin with capital letters.

Writing Activity 18: Summary
(Only the Main Ideas)

Step
1

Follow along as two passages are read aloud. The first passage is a report titled "Fighting Fires." The second passage is a summary of "Fighting Fires."

Fighting Fires

Firefighters are called when there is a fire that is too big to be put out by other people. When people call to say they need a fire put out, an alarm goes off at the fire station. This alarm lets the firefighters know they need to get in their trucks and go to the fire.

Fire trucks are not like normal trucks. You have probably seen one before. They are long and red. They carry hoses and ladders. There is also a special truck that holds a large tank of water. Firefighters use the tank of water to start putting out a fire. Other firefighters look for fire hydrants. Fire hydrants can be found on streets and near buildings. The fire hydrants are connected to pipes that hold water. Firefighters hook their hoses to the hydrants. Then, they turn on the hydrants. Water shoots through the hoses and helps firefighters put out fires.

When the firefighters get to a fire, the firefighter who is in charge looks around to see what is happening. Then, he tells the other firefighters what they need to do. Some put out the fire, and others might have to help rescue people. Firefighters are very brave people. Fire fighting is an important job that helps keep people safe.

by Lainie Burke

Step

1

continued

Summary of "Fighting Fires"

Firefighters put out big fires. An alarm lets them know when it's time to go to a fire. They go to fires in their trucks. The trucks have hoses and ladders. Firefighters use water to put out fires. They connect their hoses to special trucks and to fire hydrants. This is where the water comes from. When firefighters get to a fire, they put out the fire and help save people. Firefighters are brave. Their job is important.

Step

2

Remember, a good summary (only the main ideas) has the following parts.

- main ideas
- no unimportant or unnecessary information
- a small amount of detail
- my own words

Step

3

Use the following idea to plan your summary (only the main ideas).

Read the report titled "Frogs" on page 125. Write a summary (only the main ideas).

Step
3
continued

Frogs

Frogs live both in water and on land. They have to stay near fresh water. They cannot survive in salt water. Frogs are good swimmers and jumpers. They have long, muscular back legs to help them jump. Most frogs have four webbed feet. These help them swim.

Frogs are coldblooded. This means their body temperatures are the same as the air temperature around them. They have to look for cool, shady places to rest if they become too hot. Frogs look for warm, sunny places if they are too cold.

Frogs have backbones. Their eyes bulge out from their faces. They can see in most directions without turning their heads. The skin of a frog is smooth and slightly damp. Frogs have teeth in their upper jaws and no teeth in their lower jaws. Frogs use their long, sticky tongues to catch bugs. They swallow their food whole.

Step
4

Use your planning guide and graphic organizer to help you think through your summary (only the main ideas). You can use pictures or words to plan your summary (only the main ideas).

STEPS FOR WRITING A SUMMARY

Planning Guide for Including Only the Main Ideas

Topic: _____

Complete the Following Steps:

Step
1
❏ **Skim the reading selection and begin to look for the main idea.**

Step
2
❏ **Underline the topic sentence for each paragraph in the text selection.** (If there is no topic sentence, write one for the paragraph.)

Step
3
❏ **Cross out unimportant information in the text selection.**

Step
4
❏ **Cross out information that is repeated.**

STEPS FOR WRITING A SUMMARY

Graphic Organizer Including Only the Main Ideas

Topic: _____

Write what the text selection is about. Include only important information.

Beginning:

Main Idea:

Ending:

Write your summary.

Writing Activity 18

Step

5

_____

- -

_____

- -

_____

- -

_____

- -

_____

- -

_____

- -

_____

- -

_____

- -

_____

- -

_____

If you need more room, ask a parent or a teacher for another piece of paper.

Step

6

The checklist shows what your best paper must have. Use the checklist below to review your work.

Checklist for Writing Activity 18

❑ My summary includes only important information.

❑ My summary starts at the beginning.

❑ My summary states the main idea.

❑ My summary has an ending.

❑ My summary does not include information that is not important.

❑ My sentences end with a period, an exclamation point, or a question mark.

❑ My sentences begin with capital letters.

Writing Activity 19:
Thank-You Note

Step Follow along as the thank-you note is read aloud.

1

samantha the snake

April 20, 2002

Dear Mrs. Coulis,

Thank you for coming to visit our class. We enjoyed meeting Samantha the snake. We learned that snakes are interesting creatures. We will always remember how friendly Samantha was to us.

Please thank Samantha for us, too.

Sincerely,

Mr. Sartin's Class
Westbrook Elementary School

Step
2

Remember, a good thank-you note has the following parts.

- the date
- a greeting
- a body
- a closing
- a signature

Step
3

Use the following idea to plan your thank-you note.

> **You received a special gift. Write a thank-you note to the person who gave you the gift. Explain why you are thankful.**

Step
4

Use your planning guide and graphic organizer to help you think through your thank-you note. You can use pictures or words to plan your thank-you note.

THANK-YOU NOTE

Planning Guide

Date | Month, Day, Year

Greeting
Dear Mr., Ms., Mrs., or Dr. _____,
Dear Aunt or Uncle,
Dear Grandmother or Grandfather,
Dear (friend's name),

Body

What are you thankful for?

- a gift (a toy, money, someone's time)
- a kindness shown to you
- a special trip
- someone's visit to your home or classroom
- someone who saw your performance or work
- a special privilege from a teacher or principal
- a place you went on a field trip

Explain why you are thankful in your own words.

I liked the gift because _____.
I learned that _____.
I appreciated your kindness because _____.

Closing comment

I hope to see you soon.
We will always remember _____.
I hope you can visit.

Closing
Your nephew or niece,
Your grandson or granddaughter,
Your friend,
Sincerely,
Love,

Signature
(Your Name)

THANK-YOU NOTE

Graphic Organizer

Date:

Greeting:

Body: What are you thankful for?

Explain why you are thankful.

Closing comment

Closing:

Signature:

Write your thank-you note.

Writing Activity 19

Step

5

If you need more room, ask a parent or a teacher for another piece of paper.

Step
6

The checklist shows what your best paper must have. Use the checklist below to review your work.

Checklist for Writing Activity 19

❑ I use the form for a letter.

❑ My thank-you note tells my reader what I am thankful for.

❑ My thank-you note explains why I am thankful.

❑ My thank-you note includes an ending.

❑ I try to spell words correctly.

❑ My sentences end with a period, an exclamation point, or a question mark.

❑ My sentences begin with capital letters.

Writing Activity 20:
Thank-You Note

Step Follow along as the thank-you note is read aloud.

1

January 1, 2003

Dear Aunt Martha,

   Thank you for sending me the special hat. I think it is really neat that you made the hat yourself. You are very talented. No one in my class has a hat like it. I tell everyone you made it for me. I think some of my friends would like you to make them hats, too. I hope you can visit our family soon.

Love your niece,

Eileen

Step
2

Remember, a good thank-you note has the following parts.

- the date
- a greeting
- a body
- a closing
- a signature

Step
3

Use the following idea to plan your thank-you note.

Write a thank-you note to someone in your school for something special he or she taught you or did for you. Some people you may want to consider thanking include a teacher, a principal, a bus driver, a custodian, a fellow student, a parent volunteer, or a cafeteria worker.

Step
4

Use your planning guide and graphic organizer to help you think through your thank-you note. You can use pictures or words to plan your thank-you note.

THANK-YOU NOTE

Planning Guide

Date

Month, Day, Year

Greeting

Dear Mr., Ms., Mrs., or Dr. _____,
Dear Aunt or Uncle,
Dear Grandmother or Grandfather,
Dear (friend's name),

Body

What are you thankful for?

- a gift (a toy, money, someone's time)
- a kindness shown to you
- a special trip
- someone's visit to your home or classroom
- someone who saw your performance or work
- a special privilege from a teacher or principal
- a place you went on a field trip

Explain why you are thankful in your own words.

I liked the gift because _____.
I learned that _____.
I appreciated your kindness because _____.

Closing comment

I hope to see you soon.
We will always remember _____.
I hope you can visit.

Closing

Your nephew or niece,
Your grandson or granddaughter,
Your friend,
Sincerely,
Love,

Signature

(Your Name)

THANK-YOU NOTE

Graphic Organizer

Date:

Greeting:

Body: What are you thankful for?

Explain why you are thankful.

Closing comment

Closing:

Signature:

Write your thank-you note.

Writing Activity 20

Step

5

_____

- -

_____

- -

_____

- -

_____

- -

_____

- -

_____

- -

_____

- -

_____

- -

_____

- -

_____

If you need more room, ask a parent or a teacher for another piece of paper.

Step
6

The checklist shows what your best paper must have. Use the checklist below to review your work.

Checklist for Writing Activity 20

❑ I use the form for a letter.

❑ My thank-you note tells my reader what I am thankful for.

❑ My thank-you note explains why I am thankful.

❑ My thank-you note includes an ending.

❑ I try to spell words correctly.

❑ My sentences end with a period, an exclamation point, or a question mark.

❑ My sentences begin with capital letters.

Chapter 5

Persuasion
(Persuasive Letter)

What is Persuasion?

The purpose of persuasion is to change how the reader thinks or feels about something. One way to persuade someone is to write a persuasive letter.

A **persuasive letter** is written to an editor of a newspaper, a teacher, a principal, a parent, or anyone else you want to persuade. Persuasive letters include information you want readers to know about. Often, these letters are written when you want to convince others about how you think or feel.

- You tell your thoughts and feelings.
- You give reasons.
- You tell them what you want to have happen.

Writing Activity 21:
Persuasive Letter

Step

1

Follow along as the persuasive letter is read aloud.

September 13, 2002

Dear Mr. Williams,

I think students should be able to bring drinks to school. As you know, we do not have air conditioning, and our school can be very hot. On hot days, students get very thirsty. Our teachers give us drinking fountain breaks. Sometimes we get thirsty in between these breaks. If we could have drinks in class, we would not have to worry about breaks.

Not all students like water. If they brought their own drinks, they could bring what they like. If we all brought our own drinks, we would not have to worry about germs. My mom told me there are germs on the drinking fountain. When students stay away from germs, they do not get sick as often.

Please change the school rule. Let students bring drinks to school. This way, we will not be thirsty on hot days.

Sincerely,

Sophie Ruiz

Step
2

Remember, a good persuasive letter has the following parts.

- a date, a greeting, a body, a closing, and a signature
- a statement of your opinion
- facts that support your opinion
- a conclusion that restates your opinion

Step
3

Use the following idea to plan your persuasive letter.

Write a persuasive letter to your principal about something you think needs to be changed in your school.

Step
4

Use your planning guide and graphic organizer to help you think through your persuasive letter. You can use pictures or words to plan your persuasive letter.

PERSUASIVE LETTER

Planning Guide

Date

Month, Day, Year

Greeting

Dear Mr., Ms., Mrs., or Dr. _____,
Dear Mom or Dad,
Dear Teacher or Principal,
Dear (friend's name),

Body

Why are you writing?

- to give an opinion about something
- to suggest a change
- to persuade someone

Important reasons to support your opinion:

- I think that . . .
- I believe that . . .
- In my opinion . . .

What do you want to happen?

- In conclusion . . .
- In summary . . .
- I would like you to think about _____.

Closing

Your son or daughter,
Your student,
Your friend,
Sincerely,
Yours truly,
Thank you,

Signature

(Your Name)

PERSUASIVE LETTER

Graphic Organizer

Date:

Greeting:

Why are you writing?

Why should readers support your opinion?

What do you want to happen?

Closing:

Signature:

Write your persuasive letter.

Writing Activity 21

Step

5

If you need more room, ask a parent or a teacher for another piece of paper.

Step
6

The checklist shows what your best paper must have. Use the checklist below to review your work.

Checklist for Writing Activity 21

❑ I tell what I am writing my persuasive letter about.

❑ My letter gives reasons why I believe my opinion is important.

❑ In my conclusion, I say what I would like to happen.

❑ I use the form for a letter, including:
- a date,
- a greeting,
- a body,
- a closing, and
- a signature.

❑ My sentences end with a period, an exclamation point, or a question mark.

❑ My sentences begin with capital letters.

Writing Activity 22:
Persuasive Letter

Step

1

Follow along as the persuasive letter is read aloud.

April 15, 2002

Dear Ms. Peters,

I am writing to tell you I believe the school library needs to stay open during the summer months. There is no library in our neighborhood. Many children have no way to get to the library on the other side of town.

If our school library were open, children would have something to do. Reading helps us learn. Right now, instead of learning, many kids get into trouble.

Since the school is in our neighborhood, we could walk to the school library. We would have no problem getting there. I think this would be good for all kids in the area.

Please talk to the people in charge of the school library. Let them know the students would like it if the library were open during the summer months.

Sincerely,

Keith Clark

Step Remember, a good persuasive letter has the following parts.

2
- a date, a greeting, a body, a closing, and a signature
- a statement of your opinion
- facts that support your opinion
- a conclusion that restates your opinion

Step Use the following idea to plan your persuasive letter.

3

> **Write a persuasive letter to your teacher. Persuade your teacher to let your class have extra time for recess.**

Step Use your planning guide and graphic organizer to help you think through your persuasive letter. You can use pictures or words to plan your persuasive letter.

4

PERSUASIVE LETTER

Planning Guide

Date

Month, Day, Year

Greeting

Dear Mr., Ms., Mrs., or Dr. _____,
Dear Mom or Dad,
Dear Teacher or Principal,
Dear (friend's name),

Body

Why are you writing?

- to give an opinion about something
- to suggest a change
- to persuade someone

Important reasons to support your opinion:

- I think that . . .
- I believe that . . .
- In my opinion . . .

What do you want to happen?

- In conclusion . . .
- In summary . . .
- I would like you to think about _____.

Closing

Your son or daughter,
Your student,
Your friend,
Sincerely,
Yours truly,
Thank you,

Signature

(Your Name)

PERSUASIVE LETTER

Graphic Organizer

Date:

Greeting:

Why are you writing?

Why should readers support your opinion?

What do you want to happen?

Closing:

Signature:

Write your persuasive letter.

Writing Activity 22

Step

5

_____

- -

_____

- -

_____

- -

_____

- -

_____

- -

_____

- -

_____

- -

_____

- -

_____

- -

_____

- -

_____

If you need more room, ask a parent or a teacher for another piece of paper.

Step
6

The checklist shows what your best paper must have. Use the checklist below to review your work.

Checklist for Writing Activity 22

❑ I tell what I am writing my persuasive letter about.

❑ My letter gives reasons why I believe my opinion is important.

❑ In my conclusion, I say what I would like to happen.

❑ I use the form for a letter, including:

- a date,
- a greeting,
- a body,
- a closing, and
- a signature.

❑ My sentences end with a period, an exclamation point, or a question mark.

❑ My sentences begin with capital letters.

Thank You
For Your Purchase!

Also Available:

Write on Target for Grades 3/4

Write on Target for Grades 5/6

Read on Target for Grades 3/4

Read on Target for Grades 5/6

For more information on our products, call 1-877-PASSING (toll free), or visit

www.showwhatyouknowpublishing.com